Could We Live on the Moon?

By Frieda Wishinsky

CELEBRATION PRESS
Pearson Learning Group

Contents

The Moon   3

Air   6

Water   8

Food   10

Weather   14

Gravity   18

Life on the Moon?   20

Recommended Reading   22

Glossary   23

Index   24

The Moon

Have you ever looked at the Moon and wondered what it would be like to live there? Many people have. They wonder if someday people from Earth could live on the Moon.

Over the years scientists have discovered a lot about the Moon. They've used **telescopes** to study it. People have even traveled to the Moon and back. In July 1969, U.S. **astronauts** Neil Armstrong and Edwin "Buzz" Aldrin became the first people to set foot on the Moon.

The astronauts started their journey to the Moon in this rocket. ▶

◀ The astronauts landed on the Moon's surface in the *Eagle*, a **lunar module**

More astronauts went to the Moon after that.
They spent hours exploring. They collected
Moon rocks and soil to study.

We now know that the Moon is very different
from Earth. We also know that people can survive
on the Moon for a short time. If people can visit
the Moon, could they live there? Does the Moon
have the things people need to live?

Astronauts used tools to collect
rocks and soil from the Moon.

Air

People need air to breathe. Air is a mixture of **gases** that surrounds our planet. One of the gases in air is **oxygen**. Oxygen is a gas our bodies need to stay alive. On Earth there is plenty of air for us to breathe. It's all around us.

The Moon doesn't have air around it like Earth does. There is no air for people to breathe. Astronauts had to carry oxygen with them to the Moon.

When astronauts walked on the Moon, they wore a backpack that contained oxygen.

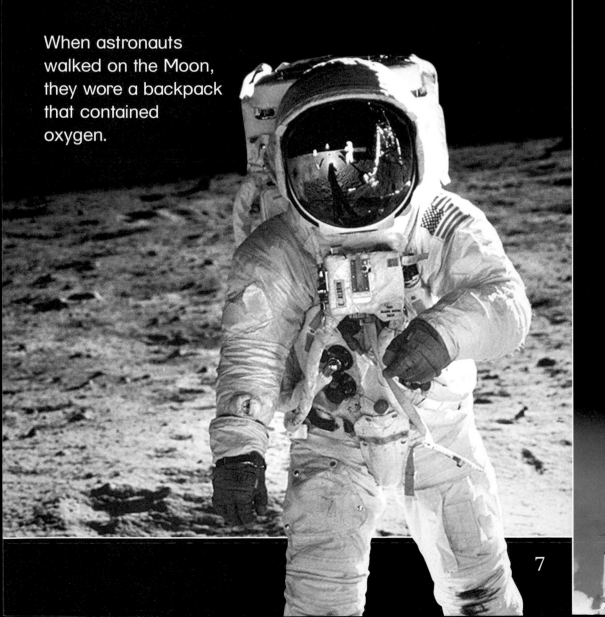

Water

People and animals need water to survive. Plants need water to survive, too. Most of the Earth's surface is made up of oceans, lakes, and rivers.

Water has never been found on the Moon. Some scientists think there may be frozen water at the Moon's north and south poles. They want to learn more about that. For now, people would need to bring water from Earth to live on the Moon.

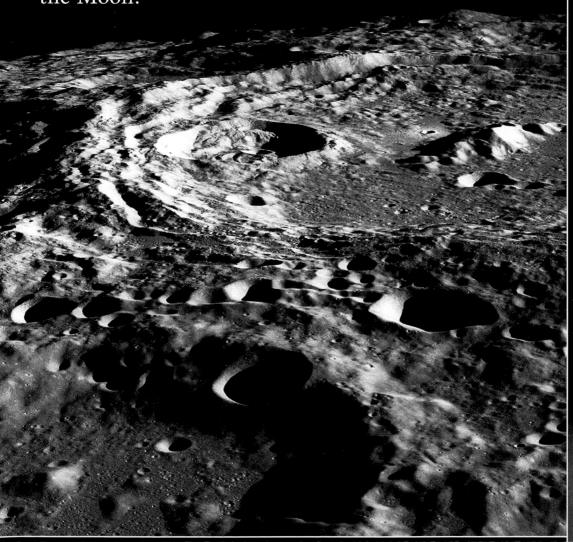

Food

People need food to live. Without water and air, however, no plants or animals can survive to produce food. Since there is no food on the Moon, astronauts had to bring all their food with them.

sandwiches

fruit drink

These are some of the foods astronauts brought to the Moon.

Astronauts on later space missions used
this serving tray to heat their food.

It would be hard for people planning to live
on the Moon to transport all the food they
would need. It would be too much to carry.
People would have to figure out how to make
their own food on the Moon.

Since the early days of space flight, scientists have tried to grow food in space. Astronauts have grown plants inside their **spacecraft**. These are some of the plants they've grown.

bean ▲

▲ wheat

soybean ▶

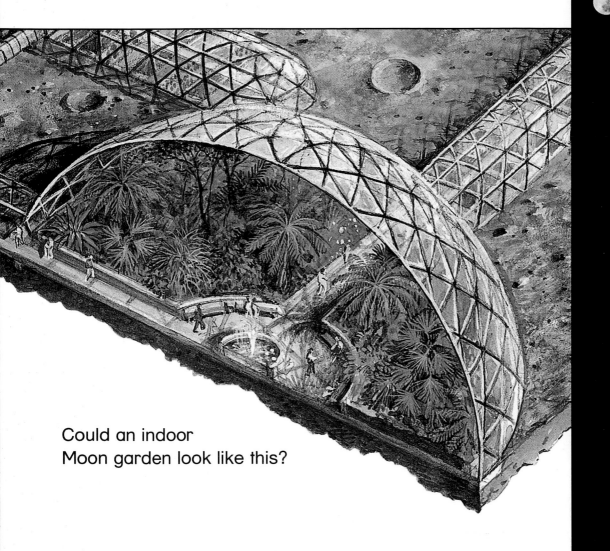

Could an indoor
Moon garden look like this?

Scientists think that fresh food may be grown indoors on the Moon someday. This would help people who want to live there. They wouldn't have to bring food with them to the Moon. Instead, they could grow their own food.

Weather

Weather is what the air outside is like. Plants and animals need weather that's not too hot and not too cold. Most need sunshine and rain.

hot and little rain　　　　　　　　**warm and some rain**

The weather is always changing on Earth. Sometimes it's warm and sunny. Sometimes clouds block the Sun. Sometimes the wind blows and rain falls. Humans can live in nearly every kind of weather on Earth.

cold and snow

On the Moon there is no weather because there is no air. There are no clouds to block the Sun. There is no wind to blow dust around. Not one raindrop falls.

This astronaut's footprint may remain on the Moon for millions of years.

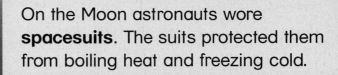

On the Moon astronauts wore **spacesuits**. The suits protected them from boiling heat and freezing cold.

Because there is no weather, **temperatures** on the Moon can be much hotter and colder than Earth temperatures. During the daytime the Moon is hotter than boiling water. At night it's much colder than Antarctica, the coldest place on Earth.

Gravity

Our Earth has **gravity**. Gravity is a force. It pulls things down toward Earth.

Gravity brings a ball back down when we throw it up. It pulls an apple that falls from a tree to the ground. It keeps our feet on the ground.

When astronauts walked on the Moon, they felt light and bouncy. That's because gravity on the Moon isn't as strong as Earth gravity. The Moon's gravity didn't pull on things as much.

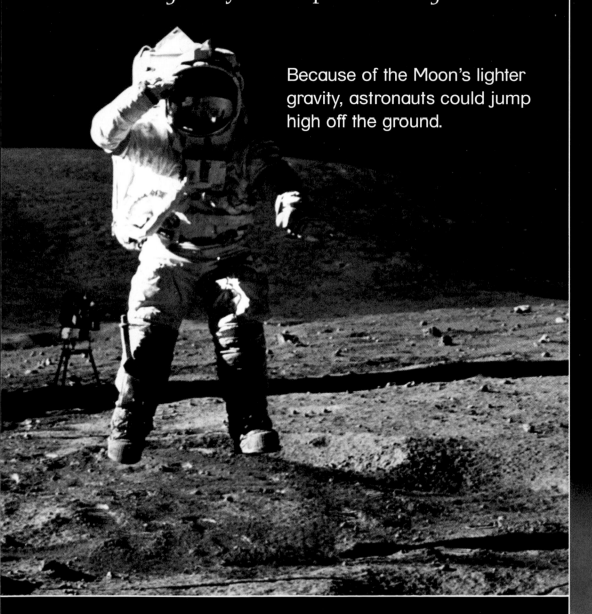

Because of the Moon's lighter gravity, astronauts could jump high off the ground.

Perhaps we could live on the Moon someday. What do you think? Would you want to?

What would your Moon home look like?

Recommended Reading

These books and Web sites will help you learn more about the Moon.

The Moon Book
by Gail Gibbons
Holiday House, 1997

*Spacebusters:
The Race to the Moon*
by Philip Wilkinson
Dorling Kindersley, 1998

What the Moon Is Like
by Franklyn Mansfield Branley
HarperCollins, 2000

Astro for Kids Moon page:
http://www.astronomy.com/content/static/AstroForKids/Moon.asp

NASA home page (Kids' area):
http://www.nasa.gov/audience/forkids/home/index.html

NASA Kids Moon page:
http://kids.msfc.nasa.gov/Earth/Moon

Glossary

astronauts	people trained to travel in space
gases	substances that are not liquid or solid
gravity	a force that pulls things toward each other
lunar module	a spacecraft that lands on the Moon
oxygen	a gas in the air
spacecraft	vehicles used to travel to and from space
spacesuits	clothes that protect astronauts
telescopes	instruments that gather light from faraway objects
temperatures	measurements that show how hot or cold things are

Index

air 6–7, 14, 16, 20

astronauts 4–5, 7, 10, 11, 12, 16, 17, 19

food 10–13, 20

gravity 18–19

spacesuits 17

temperatures 17

water 8–9, 10, 20

weather 14–17

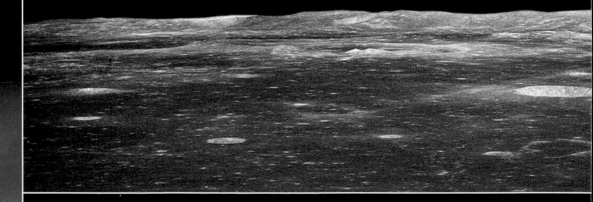